Family Life
in pictures

**Pictures
to share**

**Pictures
to share**

First published in 2010 by
Pictures to Share Community Interest Company,
a UK based social enterprise that publishes
illustrated books for older people.

www.picturestoshare.co.uk

ISBN 978-0-9563818-1-1

Front Cover:
Grandfather holding newborn twin girls. © Peter Sherrard/Photographer's Choice/Getty Images.

Front endpaper:
Family outing, family photo at the Taj Mahal, Agra, Rajasthan, northern India, Asia
© Egon Bömsch/Imagebrokers/photoshot

Rear endpaper:
A summer dinner outside. © Stephen Simpson/Taxi/Getty Images

Title page:
Five generations ranging in age from 1 month to 107. © Fox Photo's/Hulton Archive/Getty Images

Family Life
in pictures

Edited by Helen J Bate

The gift of real love

is having someone who'll
go the distance with you.

Someone who,
when the wedding day
limo breaks down,
is willing to share
a seat on the bus.

The important thing
was to love,
rather than to be loved.

Main photograph: A group of ladies looking at a new baby in an English village. © John Pratt/Hulton Archive/Getty Images

Small photograph: Mother and baby.
© Joseph McKeown/Hulton Archive/Getty Images.

Quotation: W. Somerset Maugham, 'Of Human Bondage', 1915
English dramatist & novelist (1874 - 1965)

Books

are the quietest
and most constant of friends.

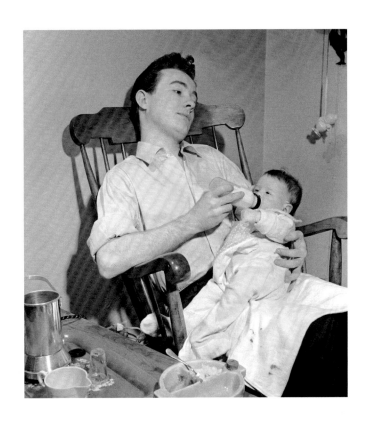

There is no
finer investment
for any community,
than putting milk
into babies.

There was a naughty boy,

And a naughty boy was he,
He ran away to Scotland,
The people for to see.

Then he found
That the ground
Was as hard,
    That a yard
    Was as long,
That a song
Was as merry,
    That a cherry
    was as red,
That lead
Was as weighty,
    That four-score
    Was as eighty,
And a door
Was as wooden
As in England.
    So he stood in his shoes,
    And he wondered,
    He wondered

He stood in his shoes
And he wondered.

Painting: Interior with woman and child (oil on canvas) by Paul Mathey,
Musee d'Orsay, Paris, France/ The Bridgeman Art Library, Getty Images

Poem: There was a Naughty Boy by John Keats (1795 - 1821)

Escaping

into the magic
of television

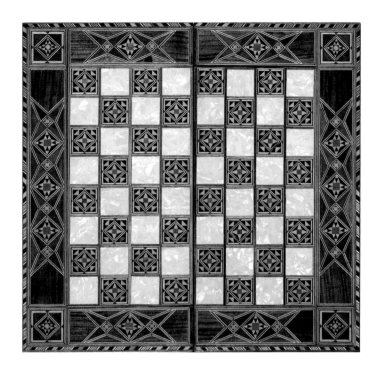

The family
that plays together,
stays together.

A little girl
enjoying a sledge ride
on the ice,

with mum
doing all the work.

Twas the night
before Christmas,
when all through the house

Not a creature was stirring,
not even a mouse.

The stockings were hung
by the chimney with care,

In hopes that St Nicholas
soon would be there.

Painting: Silent Night 1891 (oil on canvas)
by Viggo Johansen/Hirschsprungske Samling/
Copenhagen/Denmark /
The Bridgeman Art Library/ Getty Images

Quotation: From poem by
Clement Clarke Moore (1779 - 1863)

A family
gets together

to sing old songs

It is the height
of a Minnesota winter,
and snow has made
travel impossible.

Show me the way to go home

I'm tired and I want to go to bed

I had a little drink about an hour ago

And it's gone right to my head...

When I walk
into my kitchen today,

I am not alone.

Whether we know it or not,
none of us is.

We bring fathers and mothers
and kitchen tables,
and every meal we have ever eaten.

Food is never just food.
It's also a way of getting
at something else:

who we are,
who we have been,
and who we want to be.

I remember washing up

as the best time of family life.

Photograph: Men washing up. © Lambert/
Archive Photo's/Hulton Archive/Getty Images

Quotation: Lady quoted in article by Virginia Ironside,
The Independent. 27th October 1995.

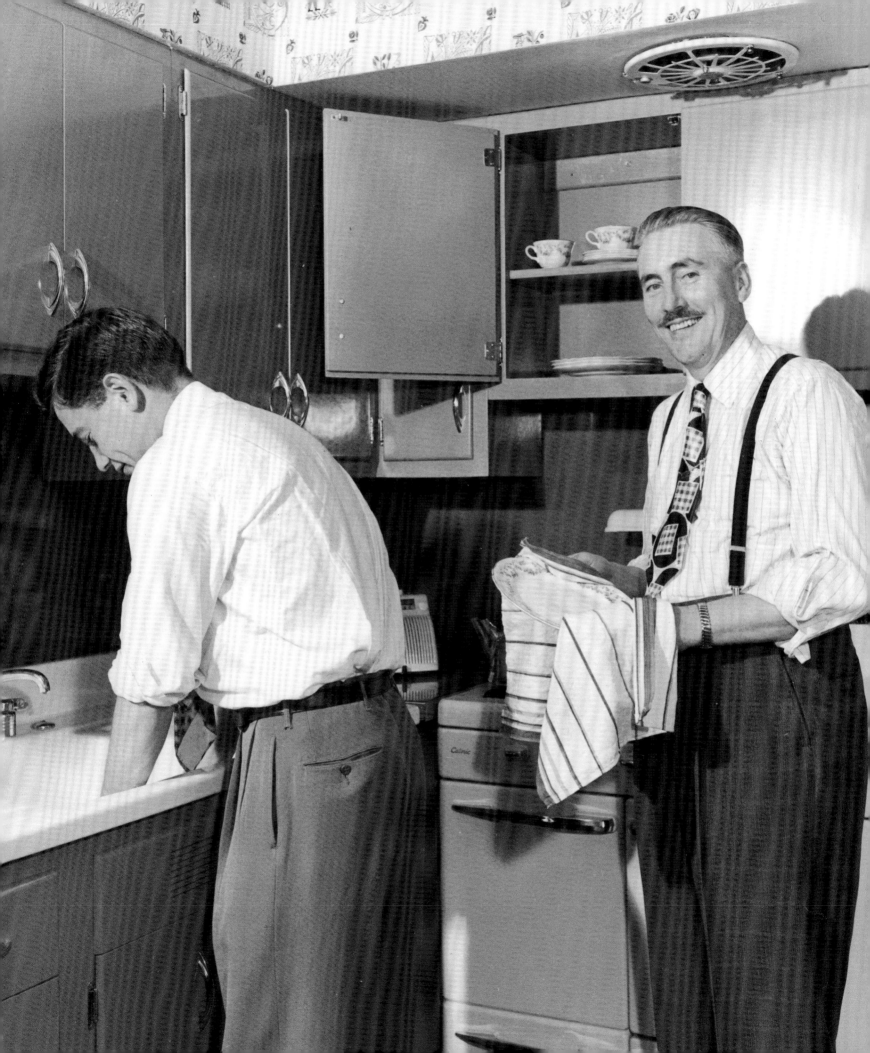

The Family (1932)

The artist Bernard Fleetwood-Walker
painted this picture of himself
with his first wife 'Mickey',
and their two sons, Colin and Guy.

Bernard Fleetwood-Walker was born in 1893
in Birmingham, a twin and one of five children.

During the First World War he served in France
as a sniper in the Artist's Rifles,
a volunteer regiment of the British Army.

Returning to Birmingham after the war
he married Marjorie White ('Mickey') in 1920.

Painting: The Family, c.1932 (oil on canvas) by Bernard Fleetwood-Walker (1892-1965)
© The Potteries Museum and Art Gallery, Stoke-on-Trent, UK/ The Bridgeman Art Library
See the artist's work at www.fleetwood-walker.co.uk

O Lord my God,
When I in awesome wonder,

Consider all the works
Thy hands have made;

I see the stars,
I hear the mighty thunder,

Thy power throughout
the universe displayed.

Then sings my soul,
My Saviour God,
to Thee,

How great Thou art,
How great Thou art!

Photograph: A family in church. Superstock/Getty Images

Quotation: Words from the popular hymn 'How Great Thou Art'.

Triplets,

Elaine, Evelyn and Linda Wilson,
celebrating their birthday
with a cake and candles.

A nursemaid

takes a line of young,
identically dressed children
for a walk in the local park.

Her small charges are
from Hutchinson House children's home
in London.

If more of us
valued food
and cheer
and song
above hoarded gold,

it would be
a merrier world.

The telephone
is the world's most popular
means of communication.

The first long distance telephone call
was made in 1915.

The rotatory dial was invented in 1923
The cordless phone was invented in 1965
The mobile phone was invented in 1983

Some are
kissing mothers

and some are
scolding mothers,

but it is love just the same.

Photograph: Mother and daughter
© David C Ellis/Stone+/Getty Images

Quotation: Pearl Buck, quoted in O Magazine, May 2003
US novelist in China (1892 - 1973)

Love is an act of endless forgiveness,

a tender look which becomes a habit.

Quotation: Peter Ustinov
English actor & author (1921 - 2004)

I'm forever blowing bubbles

Pretty bubbles in the air.

Quotation: From the popular song of 1918

Main photograph: Two small children watching their grandmother blow bubbles. © J Duckworth/Hulton Archive/Getty Images

Small photographs: istockphoto

Pictures to share

Acknowledgements
Our thanks to the contributors who have allowed their
imagery to be used for a reduced or no fee.

Graphic Design by Duncan Watts

Published by
Pictures to Share Community Interest Company.
Tattenhall, Cheshire
www.picturestoshare.co.uk

Printed in England by
Langham Press
www.langhampress.co.uk